Many underwater instructors share my opinion that skin diving, sometimes is simply referred to as snorkeling, has long been an underrated sport. The following tips will take you step-by-step through compatible equipment and techniques. These tips are designed to build a foundation from which you can develop your own capabilities.

You will find this a simple manual. You are invited to poke your face in the water and become one of us who enjoy the underwater sights, and some day will be referred to by historians as the "underwater people." Skin diving is indeed for all ages.

The equipment used in skin diving has been around for quite some time. Many advancements have been made in the equipment, making skin diving safer and more enjoyable than ever before. Many of the suggestions here would not have been possible without the equipment developed through the years by dedicated sportsmen.

Very little equipment is needed to investigate the shallow reef. The few skills necessary are simple, yet essential. Regardless of your degree of involvement, all equipment and skills have been developed for your comfort and enjoyment.

Physical fitness is important, as skin diving is a moderately strenuous sport. If you are in average shape now, after a summer of diving—you will be in great shape.

Skin diving skills form the basis of the sport of scuba. Should you decide _____ the transition would be quite natu_____ scuba (Self-contain_____ are available, each_____ There is somethin_____ would make a valu_____

Every National S_____ complete instruc_____ and a National Ce_____ is shown, your local dive shop could be _____ offer a skin diving certification. If you do enroll in a snorkeling class, I hope this simple manual will be of help. If such a program is not available, then this manual is dedicated to you! Good Luck & the Best of Diving!

Mask

Let's begin with our window to the sea, the face mask. I am sure you have experienced limited vision with the naked eye underwater. Our eyes were designed to see through air — and this air space is necessary for the eye to focus clearly. The difference in densities between air and water causes the light rays to bend (refraction) and results in the distortion and blurry vision we are all familiar with when looking underwater without the aid of a face mask. The mask provides the necessary air space for the eye to focus clearly.

Advancements in the design of the mask by the major manufacturers of diving equipment have reduced the volume of air space in the mask by bringing the faceplate closer to the eyes. The beneficial result is a greater field of vision and a better angle for viewing. With the smaller volume of air now in the mask, it is also easier for the skindiver to clear his mask and equalize the pressure in the mask while diving.

It is much easier these days to find a mask that fits well and is priced conservatively considering the effort and unbelievable expense in developing new concepts and molds.

Here's What To Look For:

1. A non-corrosive band that holds the lens securely to the rubber skirt. Our space age plastics seem to be holding up as well as stainless steel.

2. A tempered lens, affording mor strength than plate glass or plastic.

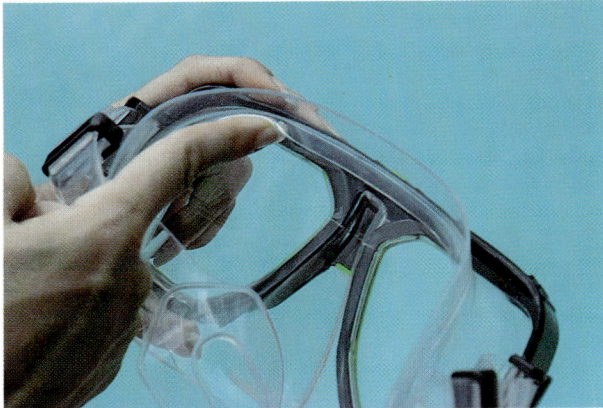

3. A double skirt, allowing a much better fit and more comfort with less chance of leakage.

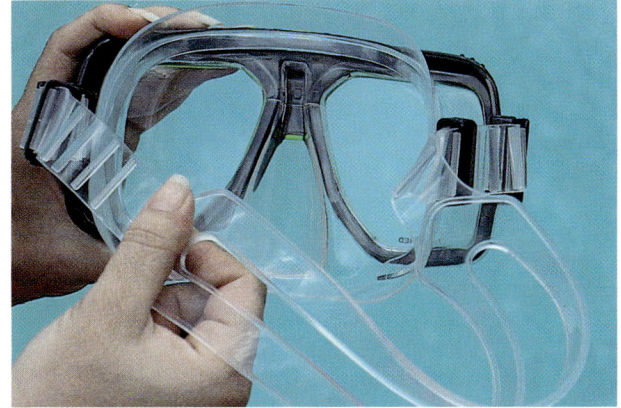

4. A split head strap that takes the pressure off the crown of your head — a discomfort often felt by the old style single strap.
New straps are emerging with oversized webbed designs to prevent traditional slippage on the back of the head. They seem to be working quite well. They are now available on some masks, or can be purchased as a replacement strap.

5. An exposed nose piece allowing you to equalize pressure in your ears easily with one hand, leaving the other hand free for holding a camera, speargun, collecting net, dive flag float, or an attractive buddy. Equalizing pressure — its techniques and skills will be discussed completely later on.

Having met the above criteria, the deciding factor on a mask is the *fit.* At this point fit becomes number one when choosing a mask — a mask that does not seal correctly (fit) out of the water will not seal correctly underwater (regardless of how tight you adjust the strap). The end result of an incorrectly fitting mask is water leaking constantly into the mask. Bearable — yes; enjoyable — no.

3

Vision is a by-product of proper fit. If you have a very small face, the lens in the mask will also be small and your field of vision will be reduced accordingly. If it makes small people feel better, they should realize that even those divers wearing masks with side windows still turn their heads to look at objects directly. No one peeks out of side windows or simply glances about underwater while holding the head perfectly still. We all turn our heads—regardless of the field of vision provided.

Fitting a mask is relatively simple. Ask a dive shop employee or friend to place the mask on your face gently. The pro will look for daylight between the skirt of the mask and your face. (If daylight shows through, the mask is not flush with the skin and any gaps will result in water leakage underwater.) If there is no daylight, inhale through your nose lightly. In doing so, the mask should seal to your face and feel secure. If a mask is airtight on the surface—it will be "water-tight" down below. A few words of caution: do not inhale too strongly when trying on a mask. You can suck a mask on your face that underwater will leak when you are not causing such an abnormal seal. Also—do not play with the skirt of the mask, pinching it to your face. You can trick yourself into the wrong mask. Go gently when choosing a proper fit. You will become accustomed to the vision offered by the mask that fits you best.

Maintenance of a face mask is also simple and quite necessary if it is going to give you years of enjoyment. Preventive maintenance is the key. Sun, salt, chlorine and suntan oil are the destructive agents.

The sun and salt can dry out the rubber in a mask in no time. Chlorine and suntan oil have devastating effects causing material breakdown in the rubber, turning your mask into a "gooey" mess. When you have used your mask in a swimming pool, ocean, etc., rinse it with fresh water and allow to dry in the shade. (The sun will damage the rubber in no time by causing it to dry out and crack.) If you've used suntan oil and there is a residue on the mask—a light dishwashing detergent and warm water will clean your mask. Followed by a light application of silicone spray or similar preservative, the life of the rubber in your mask will be increased.

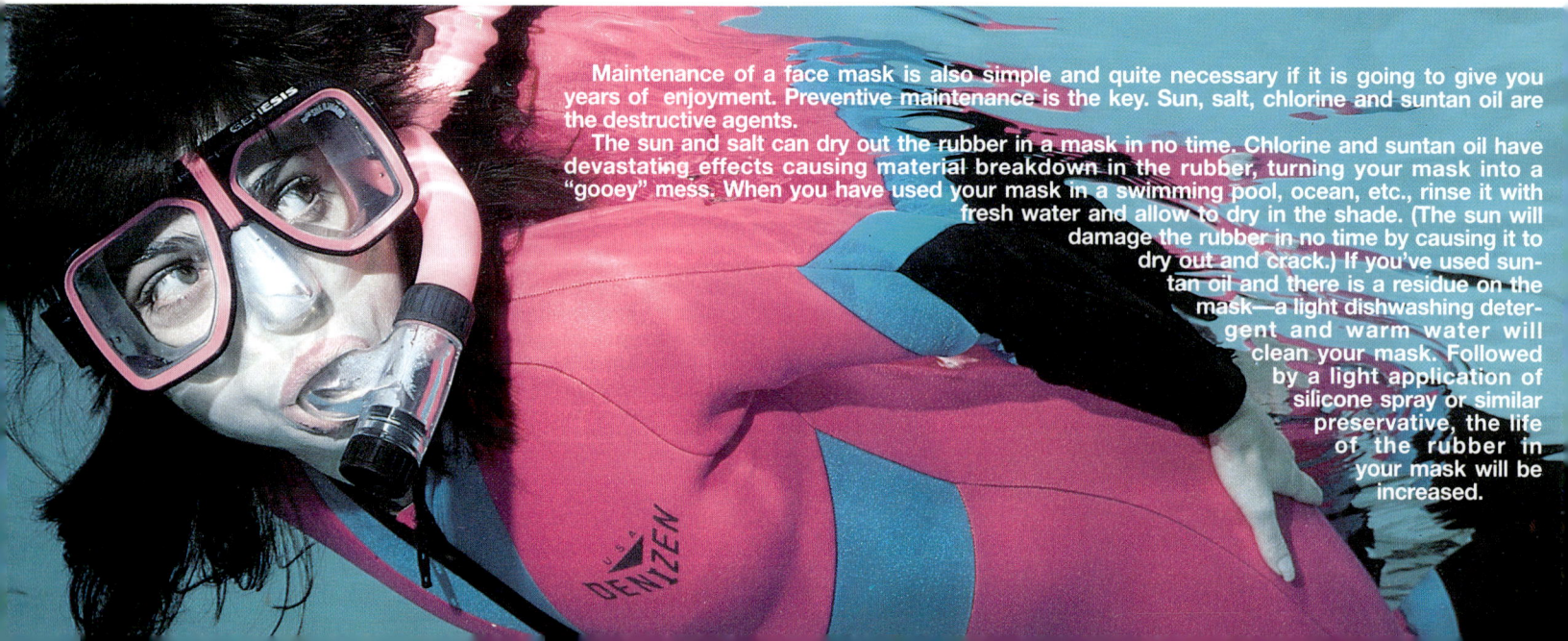

All new masks have a protective coating to preserve the mask skirt whether it be rubber, or the clear silicone material that is very popular. Enough of this coating creeps onto the lens that, unless it is cleaned thoroughly, fogging will occur while wearing the mask. "No Fog" solutions just won't work unless the lens is cleaned. Several products are now available that are specially formulated to dissolve the protective coating on the lens.

For those of you that need corrected vision and wear glasses, there exist several options to achieve corrected vision underwater. One of the more popular items is the optical mask — a mask with lenses ground into the face plate that approach your nearest diopter. You choose the mask according to the one which gives you the clearest vision. It is not your exact prescription but close enough to afford you better vision than no correction at all. It is also quite possible to have your exact prescription placed in the lens of a mask. A set of lenses is made and bonded onto the face plate of the mask. This method is usually done by the optician and will take longer whereas the dive shops carry in stock the masks with the different diopters for you to choose from. For the diver who needs corrected vision these are two of the more popular options available. Your pro shop can give you further tips as new concepts become available.

Now, let us prepare your mask for a trip to the ocean. Having scrubbed the lens and rubbed your rubber skirt down with the silicone, it is time to adjust the strap. Always undo the strap keepers and make all adjustments with your finger tips, one notch at a time. Remember, if the mask fits properly, the strap only holds it to your face. Tightening the strap in an effort to make a mask fit well will only distort the skirt further, causing additional leakage, not to mention a red ring around the face for hours. Please do not soak your mask strap with silicone spray. Silicone is very slippery.

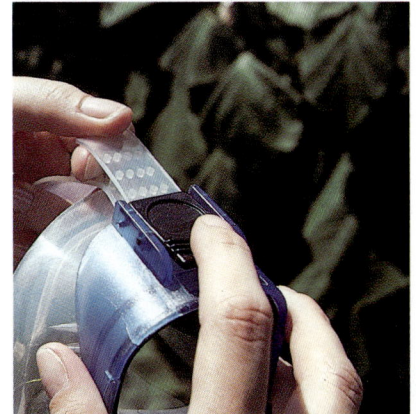

Believe it or not, there are several ways to put on a mask. Put the mask to your face, inhale, holding it to your face, then using both hands slip the strap to the crown of your head gently.

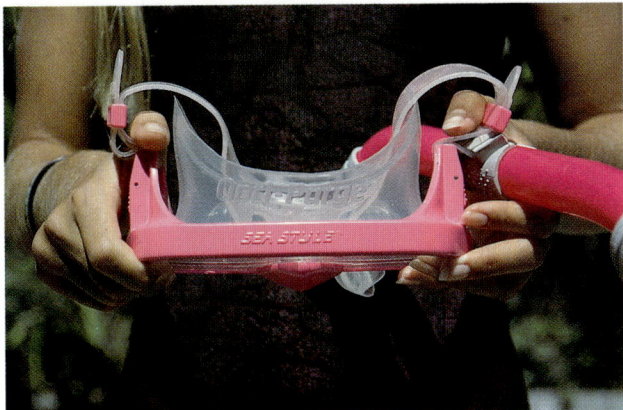

1

You can also hook your thumbs under the strap on both sides of the mask, place the split strap on the crown of your head and pull the mask gently into place. Removing all hair from the mask will insure it's not leaking for that reason. Do not hesitate to ask your buddy to check and see if all the hair is removed from the mask and give her the same con-

2

sideration.

When placing the mask on your face, be gentle and try not to destroy your strap adjustment, or worse yet, pull the metal keepers out of the mask. The straps can only take so much abuse without breaking. There are replacement straps available, however.

3

4

Once your strap is locked into place we can go on to prepare the mask with a type of "no-fog." This is a ritual performed by all divers in an attempt to retard condensation on the face plate. If a diver has a tendency to exhale through his nose into the face mask, his breath, supersaturated with moisture at body temperature, strikes a cool face plate and condenses. Fog occurs and visibility is quite limited.

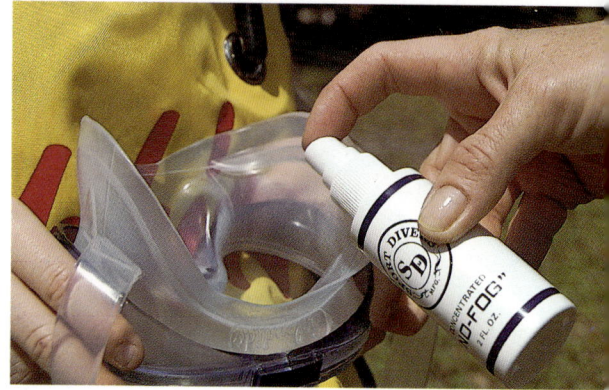

Not exhaling through the nose would help, however, w[e] are accustomed to breathing through the nose, so a bit o[f] concentration is required. Commercially prepared "No Fog[,]" works well; a few drops spread over the lens with the finger[s] and a thorough rinse with fresh or salt water will allow you t[o] fully enjoy a clear view that will last for hours.

We have tried many home remedies through the years[,] saliva, raw potatoes, baby shampoo and water, even chewin[g] tobacco, which had a desirable side benefit; no one wante[d] to borrow your mask. The commercial defoggers hav[e] brought an end to our own witches brews.

If you have chosen a mask with a purge valve, you can rest your head in the water, face down, and simply hold the mask to your face with your finger tips causing an even pressure around the skirt, tip your face in a position that places the one-way purge valve in the lowest position and exhale through your nose in the mask. One exhalation should displace the water through a large efficient purge; if not, just take another breath from the snorkel and do it again.

Earlier masks seemed to leak a lot so a technique was devised to remove the water from them as easily as possible and still be comfortable in snorkeling. The popular mustache may cause a mask to leak. I try to knife the lower skirt between my mustache and nose. This seems to work, however, I do not have a super-bushy mustache. Vaseline seems to disappear quite soon, and here comes the water.

Simply lifting the face above the water while pulling the skirt away from your face gently allows the water to run out the bottom. This should be done quickly as the weight of your head will tend to force you under.

Exercise 1
Without a purge valve

The following is a mask-clearing exercise taught in a basic SCUBA class. It is necessary to learn how to clear water from the mask while underwater. This is a great confidence builder in SCUBA as limited visibility must not alarm a diver if he is going to be comfortable in the sport. You can master this skill in less than ten minutes.

Have your buddy stand behind you to assist in keeping you stable underwater while you practice the skill. After taking a deep breath, you may be surprised how buoyant your lungs make you.

1. Tip the mask out from the top and let water in.

2. Press the top of the mask to your head causing a partial seal.

3. Tip the head up while exhaling through your nose.

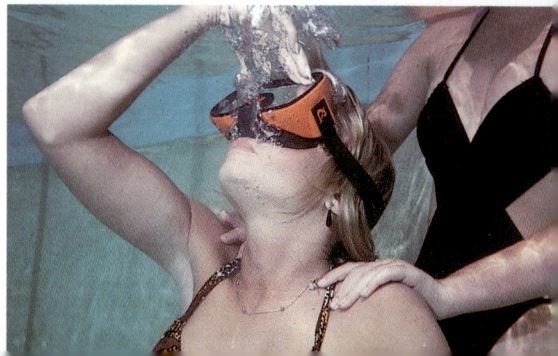

Exercise 2
With a purge valve

1. Tip the mask out from the top and let water in.
2. Hold mask to face causing a seal.
3. Tip your face down a bit to bring the purge to the bottom, and exhale through your nose.

Do not form a tendency to pull the bottom of the mask out while clearing the conventional mask. You will find yourself exhaling into the water rather than the mask. Just apply pressure to the top and go for it.

Unless you are free diving below ten feet, mask squeeze may cause you little discomfort. The cause of mask squeeze is basic. The mask was placed on your face at sea level and the air inside the mask exerts a pressure equal to one atmosphere. As you descend, additional pressure exerted by the water tends to push the mask onto your face. Exhaling slightly through the nose on occasion while descending will maintain enough pressure in the mask to eliminate eye irritation on deeper free dives.

One more tip on your face mask. Keep it on your face while you're in the water. It was designed for your convenience. If you remove it you may become inconvenienced very quickly. Replacing it while in the water can be very tricky. Save yourself the trouble and keep it on your face.

Snorkel

This innocent looking piece of equipment is no less essential to your comfort than other skin diving items designed for your safety.

The snorkel places your airway on top of your head, much like the breathing hole on a porpoise. This allows you to rest your head face down, allowing the water to support the weight of your head. Lifting the head above the surface of the water is tiring and tends to force you underwater. Try treading water with your head above water and then rest face down breathing through a snorkel. You will find snorkeling takes less energy.

Snorkel designs have changed in the past few years. The "big barrel" snorkel has helped to reduce the possibility of a carbon dioxide excess during a strenuous journey to the reef.

Without becoming too technical, understanding the respiratory system on a basic scale would help. The breath you take is transferred to the blood stream via a tender membrane (Alveoli) in the lungs. It then travels through the bloodstream to the fluid tissues where the metabolic cells accept a portion of the oxygen as fuel for the body. Waste material (carbon dioxide) is returned to the blood stream for the trip back to the lungs along with unused oxygen to be expelled through exhalation.

Although carbon dioxide is a waste material, it serves a valuable purpose. As the percentage of carbon dioxide (CO_2) builds, the tension is monitored by the brain and a signal is sent to the stretch sensors in the lungs advising you to take a breath. The process is not quite that simple, however, it may help to explain the following problem. Well over half of every breath fills a dead air space. No gas exchange is possible in the wind pipe and bronchial tubes, let alone a snorkel. We must take sufficient breath to fill these dead air spaces as well as the tender membrane traversed by the blood stream where the gas exchange takes place.

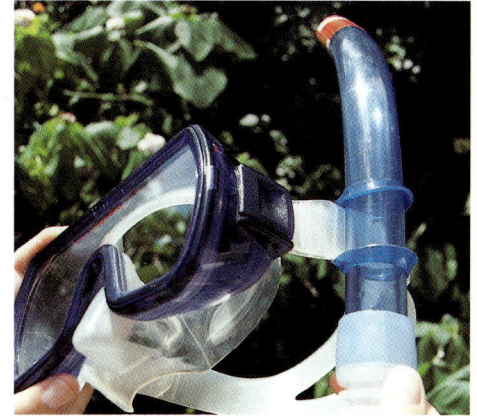

Breathing through a small snorkel can be compared to running around the block breathing through a soda straw; breathing resistance will restrict proper ventilation of the lungs. Most of us agree a snorkel should not be over 14 inches long. We have just too large a dead air space as it is, so we should add as little as possible.

Carbon dioxide will build to a point where the brain is signaling you to breathe more often, causing short rapid breaths associated with fainting — not compatible with a water sport.

In short, the big barrel snorkel has reduced this problem. Knowing your own physical limitations will reduce fatigue and proper snorkeling gear will assure you of a pleasant involvement. Stay away from devices, usually toys, that supposedly keep water out of the snorkel. They may cause traditional breathing resistance. Not all are toys, check with your pro dive shop.

There are several ways to mount the snorkel to the mask strap. If you use a conventional snorkel holder (there are several types) you will be less likely to lose the snorkel. Tucking it under the strap is not a real good idea. It can distort the mask fit, and the angle to the mouth is not quite as comfortable as you would like.

If the snorkel mouth piece causes an irritation on the inside of your mouth, do not hesitate to trim it with a pair of scissors. You can customize your mouth piece to make it more comfortable.

Which side should you mount the snorkel on? Your choice actually. Skills with the snorkeler's inflatable vest might be easier with the snorkel mounted on the right side of the mask. A SCUBA diver mounts the snorkel on the left to avoid conflict with the regulator which comes over the right shoulder. If you participate in both sports, the convenience afforded might justify switching the snorkel from one side to the other on different diving occasions.

Removing water from the snorkel while on the surface or returning from a surface dive is elementary. While face down on the surface, you simply puff stoutly and your effort will blast the water out of the snorkel. This is called the "blast method." A wise old instructor once advised his students to burst forth with a shout using the number "2" which seems to come from the pit of the stomach. This effort never failed to clear the water from the snorkel. The number 2 can be dropped once the technique is recognized.

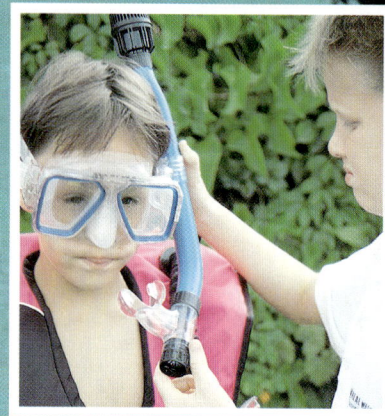

The displacement method takes a bit more practice but works well. While ascending, all good divers are looking up and reaching up while rotating a full 360 degrees to avoid collision with another skin diver, boat or dock. This good habit sets you up automatically for clearing the water from the snorkel as you reach the surface.

While looking up, the end of the snorkel is pointing down. As your face plate reaches the surface, blow into the snorkel which forces the water down and out of the snorkel with less effort than the blast method. Returning to the face down position in one motion completes the skill and raises the snorkel out of the water. Timing is important to prevent refilling the snorkel with water between your puff and returning to the face down position. Take your first breath cautiously. Practice makes perfect.

Fins

When choosing your fins, bear in mind that fins designed for snorkeling are not always compatible with SCUBA. More efficiency is required to push the additional mass and weight of SCUBA through the water. The open heel adjustable strap fin complimented by a wet suit boot can feel like part of your body. The efficiency afforded by this fin makes it quite desirable for SCUBA. If you are thinking of learning to scuba dive, the investment in this system would be wise.

The skin diver's foot size will govern the size of the closed heel fin and the resulting efficiency. The small closed heel sizes have smaller fin blades and consequently less efficiency. A wet suit boot would increase the size of the fin while affording a comfortable fit as well. A wet suit boot is required in cold water yet still has its benefits in warm water where one may have to walk over sharp rocks to reach deep enough water to snorkel in. Wearing closed heel fins for protection can be very clumsy.

There are ways to make the closed heel fins feel more comfortable. As an example, a fin size of 8–9 would be snug if you happen to have a size 9 foot; if you are a size 8, a pair of socks can take up the slack and help keep the sand out and blisters down.

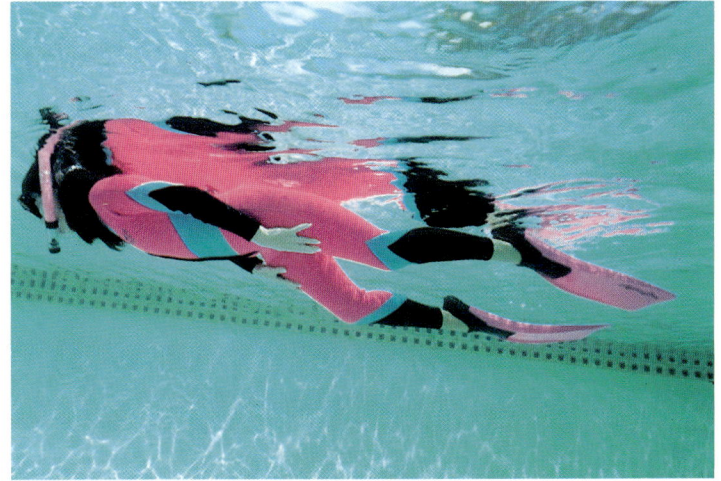

The super long fins have proven to be very efficient with a lot less effort. Swimming on the surface forces a shallow kick to prevent lifting the fin out of the water. A slow shallow kick works well with the long fins and affords unbelievable efficiency.

The key is to go slow. Fins were designed for efficiency, not speed. If you do get tired, just rest face down and enjoy the sights while your body catches up with your enthusiasm. Avoid walking on the deck with fins as much as possible. Walking backwards through the surf presents much less drag, but requires your attention to possible rocks or drop offs. Just go slow, you've got all day.

Water Pressures

Water is denser than air and therefore exerts additional pressure on the skin diver.

How does water pressure affect a diver? Much of our body is made up of fluid tissue and the pressure is simply transferred with no effect. We have bones which are rigid, and if the pressure is exerted evenly, there is no damage. The air spaces within our bodies can be squeezed by the additional pressure exerted by water.

While your lungs are not affected a great deal when free diving in shallow water, there are smaller air spaces that are: the ears, sinuses, and let us not forget the air space we placed on our face, the face mask.

This is just one other reason why swim goggles are not an accepted piece of skin diving equipment. The face mask encompassing the nose allows you to equalize pressure in the mask.

While most snorkelers enjoy the sights from the surface, many will dive below in search of new shells for their collection. Ear discomfort is not uncommon. Air spaces in our middle ear and sinuses must be equalized with surrounding water pressure to avoid discomfort.

Let's take a quick look at the mechanics of these spaces.

The external ear canal allows water to press on the eardrum which is supported by one atmosphere of pressure in the middle ear. If the eardrum doesn't get more support from the middle ear, it will begin to complain. Fortunately, it is possible to pinch off the nose and blow slightly inducing additional pressure through the eustachian tube into the middle ear. When your eardrum is not complaining, the pressure is equalized.

If a cold or allergy has you congested, the eustachian tube could be blocked and restrict the passage of air and reduce your ability to equalize pressure. Pain would be your first clue that you have failed to equalize pressure.

Remember, the eustachian tube is a muscle and can be tuned prior to dive. Pinch off your nose and practice equalizing pressure while driving to the beach. If you haven't been snorkeling for awhile this will make life a bit easier. Equalizing the sinus cavities is almost automatic if the air passages are not blocked. There's nothing like a snorkeling trip to loosen up the congestion anyway. You just won't be able to dive deep.

Just a note on earplugs. Water pressure can force them deep into the external ear canal. Enough said? A girl's swimming cap over the ears can prevent equalizing pressure as well.

FIGURE #1

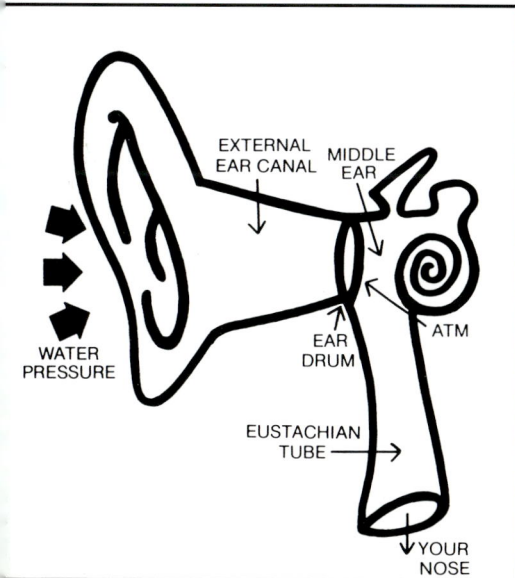

Vest

Let's take a close look at the inflatable vest as a working tool for the serious skin diver. There may be times while visiting an exotic area that a snorkeler will spend hours in the water. Resting on occasion will be a must. The inflatable vest will make this possible and add to the safety and comfort of the skin diver. Should you fill your goodie bag with shells, the additional flotation afforded by the vest will be welcomed.

The vest comes in many improved designs. A low volume vest should be adequate for snorkelers, but should not be used for SCUBA. The high volume vest, commonly known as a buoyancy compensator is designed to keep a diver and his SCUBA equipment on the surface as well as adjusting buoyancy underwater. The high volume buoyancy compensator is also compatible with skin diving.

Please understand, the vest should not be considered an emergency device. If used as a tool, it will help prevent emergencies. Let's consider the vest a working tool and develop your skills in using it as such. If you have chosen a vest with a large hose used for orally inflating and manually deflating, then the few skills will be simple.

You may want to orally inflate the vest for a swim to the reef. Give yourself a head start and put some air in the vest before you enter the water. A common error is to over inflate the vest. This will cause the snorkeler to constantly swim up on the vest, rocking from one side to the other; very strenuous. You want only a small mat under you. This will allow you to swim comfortably. The vest will lift your chest slightly which will relieve water pressure on the lungs making it a bit easier to breathe while swimming or resting.

While snorkeling you may decide to dive for a shell or simply get a closer look. It may go without saying, but you must let the air out of the vest to get underwater without a great deal of effort. If you forget it once, you won't forget it again.

Orally inflating the vest while snorkeling can be easy, or quite difficult. Let's look at the easy way:

1. Lay in the water face down breathing through the snorkel. Five minutes of practice will familiarize you with the skill.

2. Simply remove the snorkel with your right hand and place the vest oral inflator in your mouth. Push the button that opens the valve on the hose with your left hand and blow air into the vest.

3. Remember to save enough air in your lungs to clear water from your snorkel. Take a breath from the snorkel and continue the process until the vest has enough buoyancy to suit you.

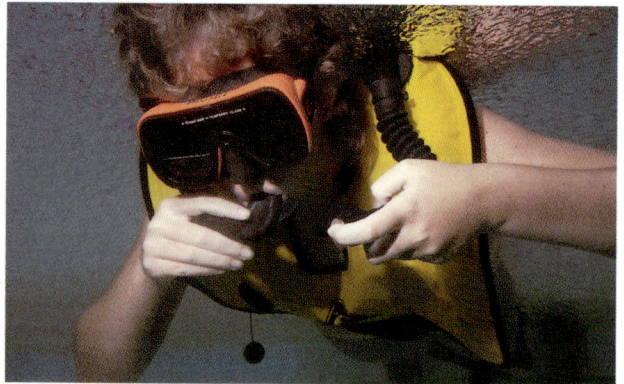

4. If you attempt to raise your head for the breath to fill the vest, the weight of your head will keep driving you underwater. This can get to be hard work right away.

Many vests come with a CO_2 cartridge and a detonator. This is often thought of as an emergency inflator. An emergency inflator, that is, if you have remembered to put a cartridge in the mechanism, recocked it for use, maintained the detonator in a rust-free manner, and examined the nylon string you plan to stake your life on to make sure it won't break when you pull on it. If the CO_2 cartridge is exposed and located next to your skin, protect yourself with a "T" shirt. When the cartridge is detonated it grows very cold. In fact, it grows cold so fast, it can cause tissue damage not unlike a burn.

Bands that hold the hoses in place should be checked to make sure they won't pull apart in use. The over pressure valve should be working. If the vest has air in it and the CO_2 cartridge is detonated, you could rip a seam without the over pressure purge working properly.

The CO_2 cartridge is a one shot deal, however, you can orally inflate the vest many times. Practice inflating and deflating the vest until you are comfortable with the skill.

OVER PRESSURE VALVE

23

Maintenance is simple yet essential. Store the CO_2 cartridge in the vest pocket or in your gear bag when not in use. If you leave it in the detonator, rust can lock it in and render it useless. Rinse the mechanism with fresh water and spray with silicone. Rinse both the inside and outside of the bag with fresh water and a cleaner designed to prevent a buildup of mildew and bacteria which accumulates inside the vest due to sea water.

Pour the solution into the inflator hose, inflate the vest, and shake vest to cover the entire inside of the bag, rinse, drain, and hang it to dry in the shade. Maintenance and care will insure a long life for the inflatible vest. Your pro dive shop will be glad to familiarize you with a snorkelers vest.

You are entitled to check your buddy's vest to familiarize yourself with the mechanism and double check his maintenance habits. If his vest is ripped or obviously corroded beyond use, he could be depending on you heavily if a crunch comes. You must make a decision to accept the responsibility or insist a working vest be worn.

It doesn't hurt to carry a whistle attached to the vest. Should you get out behind a boat in a heavy current you can get someone's attention without screaming your brains out. Inflate your vest and wait to be picked up. A long line with a float attached should be trailed behind a boat while snorkeling. This tip is a must.

Snorkeling Accessories

A few smaller items that make life easier for the skin diver include reef gloves to protect hands against coral cuts and sharp rocks. A small diver's knife can be handy where fishing line is present on the reef. A goodie bag is handy to carry your snorkeling gear and can go to the reef for collecting shells.

Protective clothing, shirt and pants, will keep the sun off your back and legs if you are going out for the first few times and have not yet developed a tan. Beware of the sun, it has ruined more than one vacation.

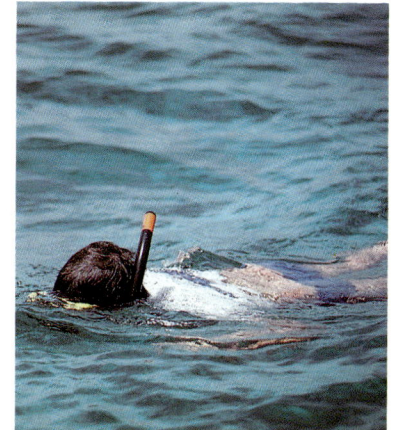

If you are wearing a wet suit for protection against the cold, a weight belt will be useful in making surface dives. Your buddy should be introduced to the quick release on the belt; he will then be able to drop it for you if a cramp should immobilize you.

While swimming on the surface in a horizontal position, your tummy will suck in a bit and sometimes allow the weight belt to travel around your waist. You could find a weight has taken the place of your buckle which has now traveled to your back. Just be aware that it can happen and check the position of the buckle from time to time. When donning the weight belt, make sure it is placed over the crotch strap if your inflatable vest has one. Many do.

Buddy System

The buddy system is as old as water sports. The old rule "never swim alone" applies to skin diving as well. Your buddy should be familiar with your equipment as well as his own. The buddy system also extends to life saving and first aid capabilities. A complete involvement in skin diving as a rewarding hobby would include a course in life saving, first aid, and CPR.

Outlining specific duties for a buddy team would not give our readers credit for intelligence or imagination. The keys are simple — awareness and consideration. Proper equipment speaks for itself. Discuss your dive plan before entering the water and assign a team leader. It's much easier to stay together if one leads and the other follows. Change roles during the trip, but stay together.

I have several tips on free diving in buddy teams. One buddy should surface dive at a time while the other buddy remains on the surface as a safety diver; he or she would then have a fresh supply of air if the diver down required assistance. Just take turns and keep an eye on each other.

Don't set up a competition with each other as to how long you can stay underwater. This is a classic mistake. You can develop your breath holding techniques without tricks. Don't overextend yourself on the bottom. The recovery time on the surface just doesn't justify the time spent on the bottom. Pace yourself. Spend a short time on the bottom to begin with; this will give you a shorter recovery time on the surface. Time and conditioning will allow you to spend more time on the bottom and shorter time on the surface. A short note on Hyperventilation is in order. First, the technique. Take as deep a breath as you can, then exhale as much as possible. Repeating this over and over is called Hyperventilation.

Hyperventilation scrubs carbon dioxide (CO_2) from the system which, if you remember, normally advises you when to take your next breath. Having scrubbed CO_2 from the system, you no longer have a gnawing urge to breathe. There is a dangerous consequence, however. The body continues to burn oxygen as fuel, and when it's gone, you simply black out. There is no warning.

I mention Hyperventilation because of the danger. Don't be tricked by using it. Conditioning is the key, not games in an attempt to remain underwater longer.

Many SCUBA certifying programs require a 50 foot underwater swim as a proficiency test. Three deep hyperventilating breaths would be in order (if needed) to pass such a test. More than three could result in your buddy having to rescue an unconscious diver — you.

Diver's Flag

The diver's flag attached to a float should be towed to your reef site. The skin diver presents a very low profile to a boater. The flag identifies the diver in the water.

The standard sport diver's flag has a red (international orange field) with a white diagonal stripe running from the top of the staff to the lower outside corner. While this flag may not be new to most boaters, enough weekenders seem to mistake the flag for a racing pylon and tempers flare unnecessarily.

The laws in most states are specific. Boaters must stay at least 100 feet away from the flag displayed on a boat or float (not a law in many states). The law also states that a diver must remain with-in 50 feet of the flag. Because of the serious risk involved, I strongly recommend the flag be towed close to the snorkeler. This would reduce the risk of making contact with a speeding boat. It would take a pretty vicious boater to run over a flag, although many come very close.

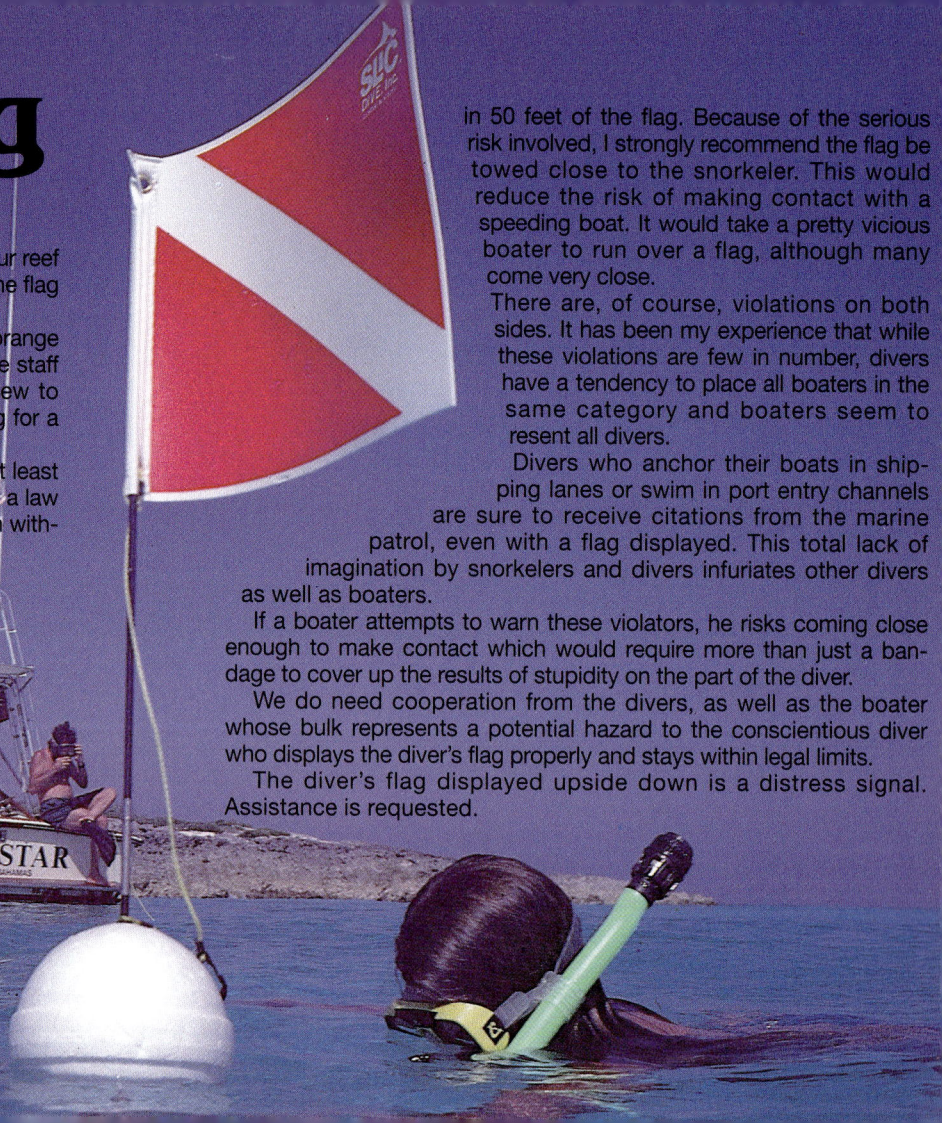

There are, of course, violations on both sides. It has been my experience that while these violations are few in number, divers have a tendency to place all boaters in the same category and boaters seem to resent all divers.

Divers who anchor their boats in shipping lanes or swim in port entry channels are sure to receive citations from the marine patrol, even with a flag displayed. This total lack of imagination by snorkelers and divers infuriates other divers as well as boaters.

If a boater attempts to warn these violators, he risks coming close enough to make contact which would require more than just a bandage to cover up the results of stupidity on the part of the diver.

We do need cooperation from the divers, as well as the boater whose bulk represents a potential hazard to the conscientious diver who displays the diver's flag properly and stays within legal limits.

The diver's flag displayed upside down is a distress signal. Assistance is requested.

Surface Dive

Surface dives may be a bit tricky, yet practicing a simple pike dive will allow you to reach the bottom with very little effort.

The pike dive begins with the skin diver in a horizontal position, moving forward slowly on the surface of the water. Arriving on the bottom is accomplished by simply bending in the middle, reaching *straight* down with one hand and lifting one leg above the surface. The weight of the leg will drive you under the surface and a few kicks will take you to the bottom.

Remember while returning to the surface the good diver is always looking up, reaching up, rotating 360° for full visibility, and set up to clear the water from the snorkel in a graceful motion. You'll feel good when you begin to feel like you belong there.

Beach & Boat Diving

There are a few techniques I can pass on to you concerning beach and boat skin diving that I have learned through experience. Some rules, so to speak, are basic common sense. All of these are backed by two laws. One of nature and one of man.

I'll refer briefly to man's law, and as extensively as the space allows discuss nature's laws. Skin diving on a controlled beach (one manned by lifeguards) may be allowed. You will, however, be expected to show good habits and adhere to the buddy system and use acceptable equipment. Lifeguards have enough problems without skin divers showing poor watermanship and diving habits. Adults as well as children can find themselves in great difficulty with inadequate equipment. An adult with too small a snorkel can render himself unconscious. A small child unattended can find the too large face mask has slipped down over the mouth and suffocates in minutes.

Many controlled beaches require a double chambered float (two tubes), one for each member of a buddy team. The float should display a diver's flag and be kept close to the team on the way to the reef. I would be surprised to see spearfishing allowed on controlled beaches. There are just too many swimmers. Where would you find a fish anyway? If you put yourself in the lifeguard's place, you just might take your good habits to a more private beach.

Now it's nature's turn. Misjudging conditions is not as easy in South Florida's eastern beaches as in many other parts of this country. Suspended particles in our shallow waters would reduce visibility to zero during a storm. Our shore line currents on a nice day are running at a fairly gentle rate. We find it easier to pick our good days in southern Florida than in many other places. In your travels, it's a good idea to check in with the pro's and find out what their ocean is all about. They will be glad to explain the character of their ocean that makes it a unique place to visit. They will advise you of currents, rips, and marine life that govern the techniques used in their area. If they offer a snorkeling trip, take it, they know where to go.

Beach patrols are usually glad to point out interesting areas on their beach. Some areas are designed and marked as good snorkeling sites.

Skin diving from the beach begins with your defogging ritual, donning fins, inflating the vest slightly, and organizing your diving flag float.

If you want to put your fins on first and then enter the water, follow this procedure; using the old figure 4 technique, hold your fin in your left hand and bring your right foot up and across your left knee. Now put your fin on. Reverse the figure 4 and repeat the exercise. Hold the fin in the right hand, bring your left foot up and across the right knee and put the fin on. You will avoid cramping with this technique so give it a try. Get your buddy to support you. Walking backwards into the water will present less drag on the shuffling fins and still allow you to watch where you are going. Most surf conditions allow you to carry the fins into the water and rest back to put them on.

If you are wearing an inflatable vest (you should be), you can put a bit of air in it for the trip to the reef. Remember to tow your diver's flag close to you and your buddy.

When snorkeling off the beach with a longshore current, it is a good idea to swim into the current while you are fresh and strong. Drifting back to end the trip will be pleasant and much less work.

If you choose to drift with the current and enjoy as much on the reef as possible, have someone follow you in a car if possible, or, be sure to take cab fare. You can cover several miles in a very short time.

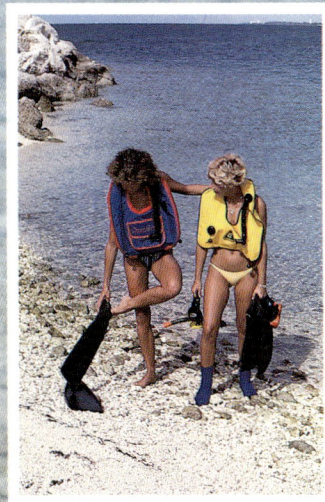

This leads us into snorkeling from a boat. Strong currents can embarrass even the seasoned skin divers. Trailing a line with a float attached is a must while anchored in a current. Cab fare won't do you any good if you are swept away, and you forgot to teach your wife how to run your boat. You'll just know you are on your way to Hong Kong. In many oceans you would be, in a very round about way. Someone who knows how to run the boat should serve as lifeguard and alarm others should anyone develop difficulties.

Displaying a diver's flag from your boat is also a must. Just remember, the bulk of your boat may draw the attention of passing boaters away from your personal diving flag towed with you. Be alert yourself and become aware of boat sounds, and glance for sail boats. We are not going to show you any gruesome pictures. Just be nice to yourself.

Many dive charter boats welcome snorkelers and are in a position to take you to areas inaccessible from the beach.

They all require an inflatable vest and good habits.

Do yourself a favor and listen to the dive master's pre-dive tips. He is advising you of depth, currents hazards peculiar to his ocean, and tips on exiting and entering his boat. No one knows these things better than the resort dive master.

Keep your gear organized in your dive bag when diving from large boats with lots of people. It's simple, take it out of your bag as you need it. After the dive, put your gear in the bag as you remove it from your body. Instant control of gear prevents loss and damage.

After the dive, clean your equipment with fresh water and a bit of maintenance. The ocean is a very corrosive mistress and will punish you for your invasion by causing your equipment to fall apart. She will have help from the ozone and the heat of the sun. Add chlorine and we complete a devastating foursome.